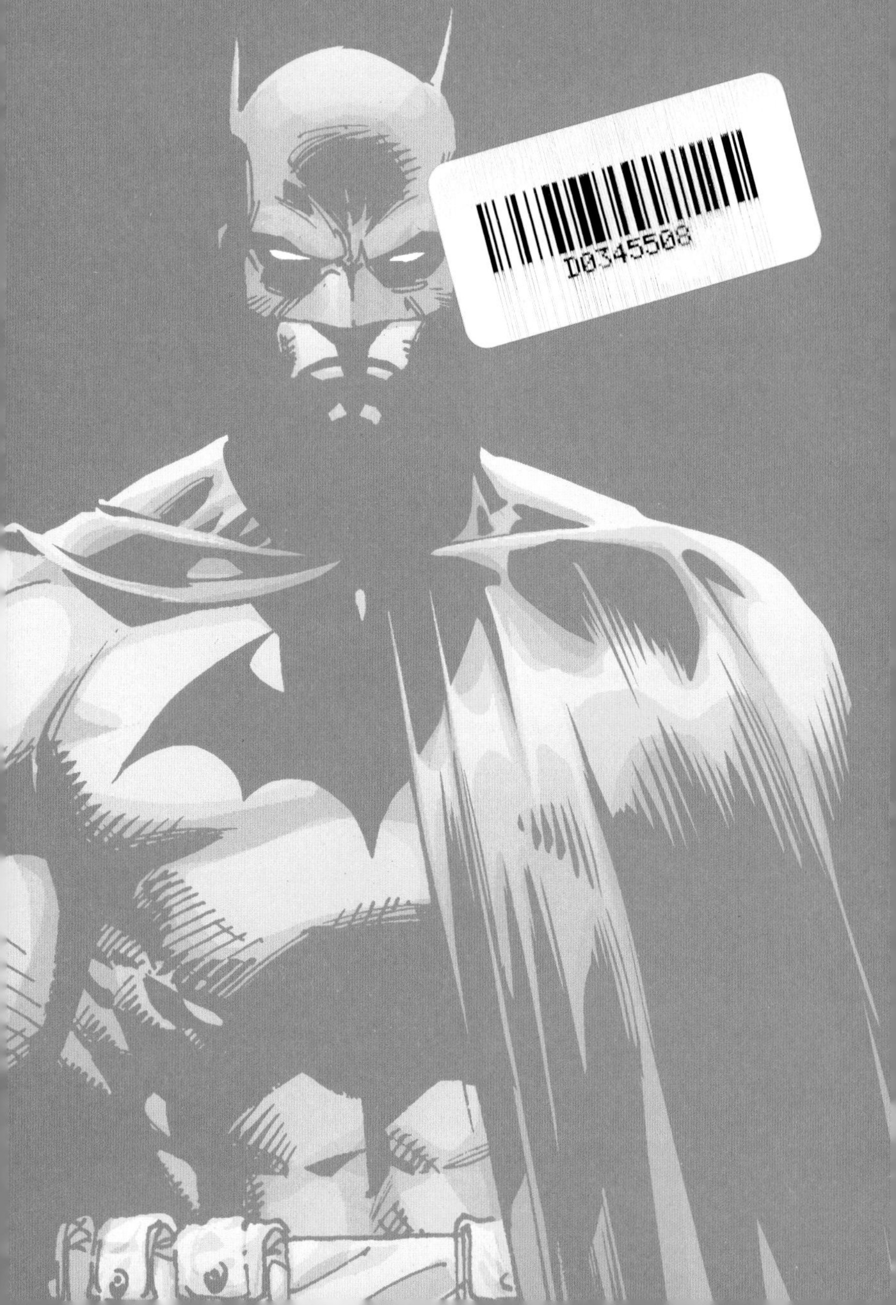

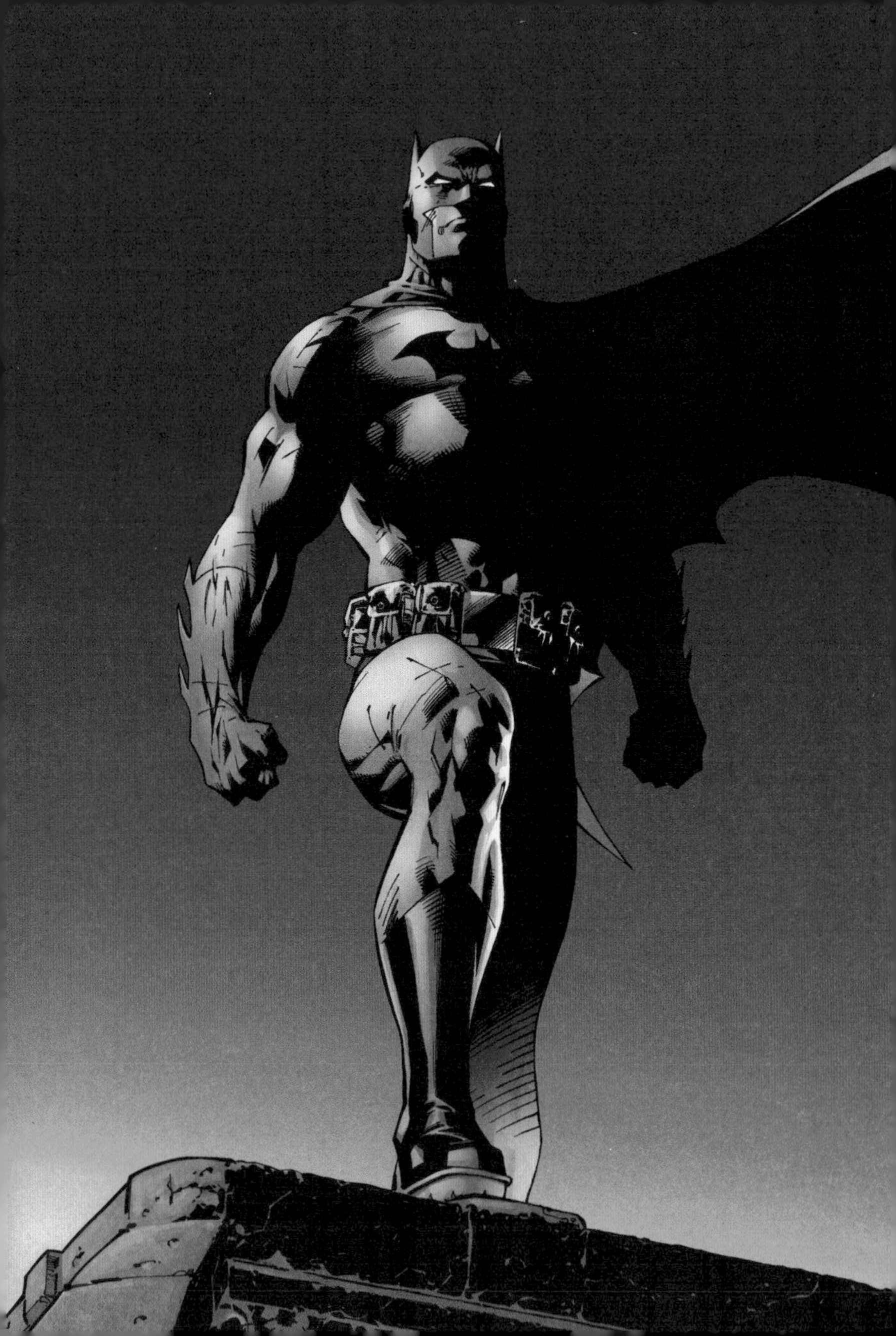

BE MORE BATMAN

WRITTEN BY GLENN DAKIN

Batman created by Bob Kane with Bill Finger

CONTENTS

ARISE, DARK KNIGHT!

Batman is one of the greatest Super Heroes of all time. And you know what's weird? He doesn't have a single power. Yep, he's just like you. All his heroism comes from inside. Superman may be faster than a speeding bullet, but even he respects Batman. Why? Because Batman has done it all himself: trained, studied, built Batcopters, and invented cool stuff like Bat-shark repellent. He is the ultimate hero, because he made it all happen himself. And you know what's even weirder? You can do the same thing. It's all in you, too. Read on and find out how, Batman fans!

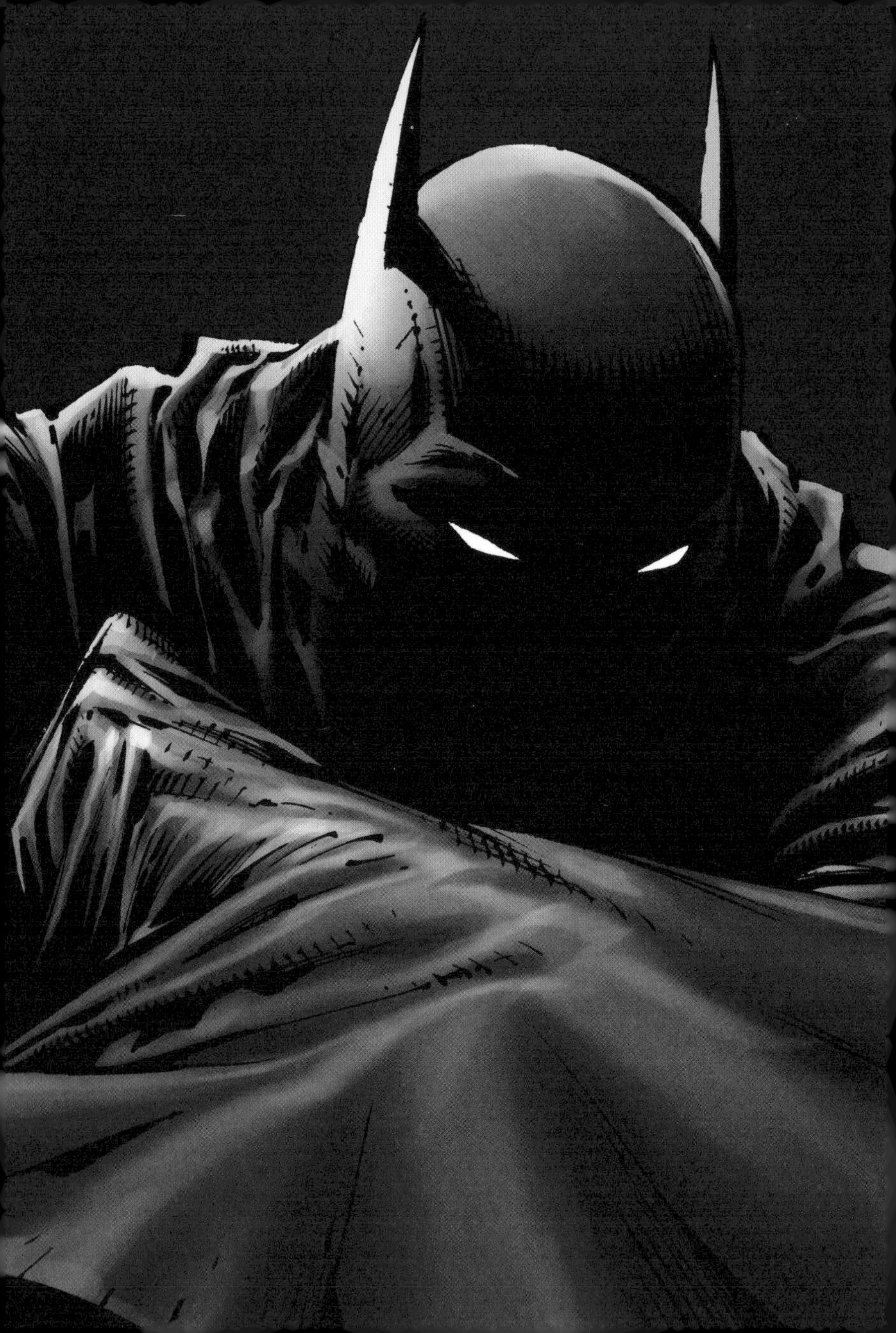

BECOME
A HERO

Today it is harder than ever to be a hero.
All the best names are already taken,
and everyone expects you to make witty
one-liners after you've defeated the villain.
Not easy. But for people like you, the true
Batman fan, there are no real obstacles to
being like Batman. Because like the Dark
Knight, you will never give up the fight.
And it starts here…

"I made a promise on the grave of my parents that I would rid this city of the evil that took their lives."

Bruce Wayne

KNOW YOUR MISSION

If you want to be a legend like Batman, then you need
to have a mission—an aim in life. If your aim is to eat
more doughnuts and sit around reading comic books,
well, that's fine. But don't expect to become a
revered figure of mystery that way. To be like the
Dark Knight, you need to choose an inspiring goal
and then aim for it like a flying Batarang.

"I became a bat.
A monster of the night."
Batman

TO CHANGE THE WORLD, CHANGE YOURSELF

When Bruce Wayne set out to fight evil, he didn't fight it as just an ordinary guy—he began by creating a striking new identity. He made the world a better place by first changing himself. You can do the same—take a look at yourself. Could you work harder, train tougher, be bolder? There are many ways to improve, and you don't *have* to dress like a giant bat to impress people (though it is kind of fun).

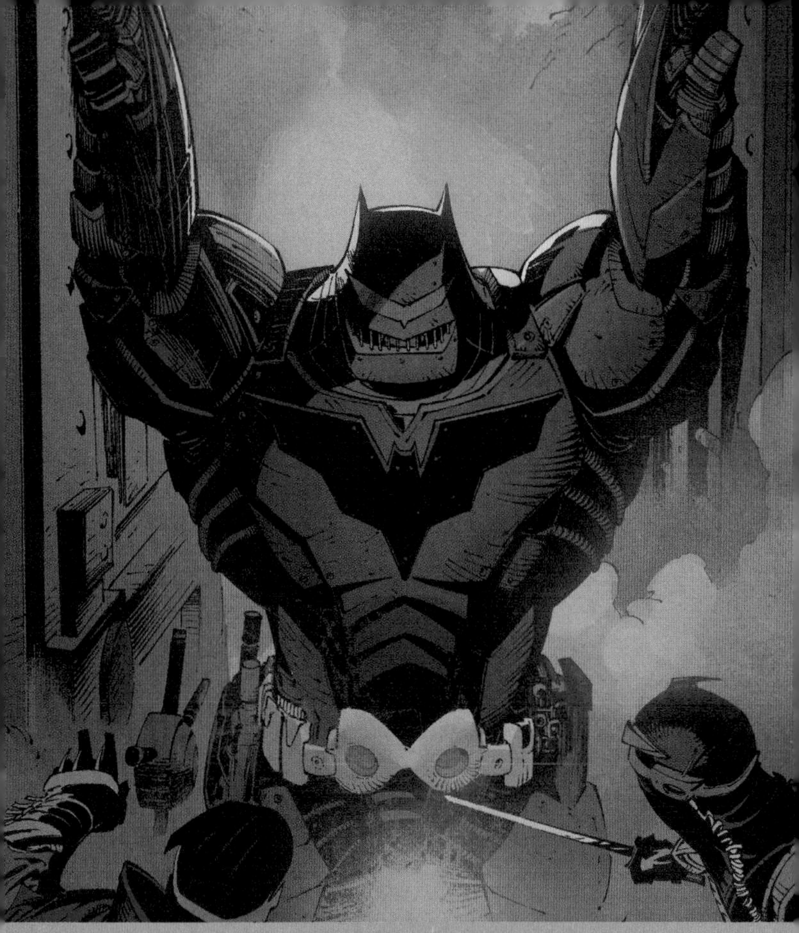

“Criminals are a superstitious, cowardly lot. So my disguise must be able to strike terror into their hearts.”

Batman

DRESS TO IMPRESS

Batman knows that to fight evil you have to look
the part. Villains will not be impressed if you turn
up to battle wearing sweatpants. Batman even has
special armors like his Thrasher suit for handling
extreme environments and home-invaders. Like
Batman, you need to look right. Dress like the
person you want to be and you'll feel like
you're halfway there.

"From this moment on, none of you are safe."
Batman

TALK THE TALK

To be like Batman, you have to talk like Batman.
Speak in short, punchy phrases, like: "It's over!"
"Give it up!" and "You're finished!" Then surprise
everyone with a complex explanation of something
that nobody else will understand: "I knew he was the
clown-napper because of the infinitesimal particles
of custard pie along the proximal nail fold of his
left index finger." People love that stuff.

"Most of the things that 'everybody knows' are wrong."
Batman

BEING MYSTERIOUS NEVER HURT

People love mysteries. Be mysterious and people will admire you. Appear out of nowhere. Vanish without saying goodbye. Never explain how you did that brilliant thing. Know things you couldn't possibly know. Say deep stuff like: "The truth is a lie." Don't apologize, don't blabber, and don't make lame jokes. Instead of explaining where you are going, just say: "I hope I'm not too late...!"

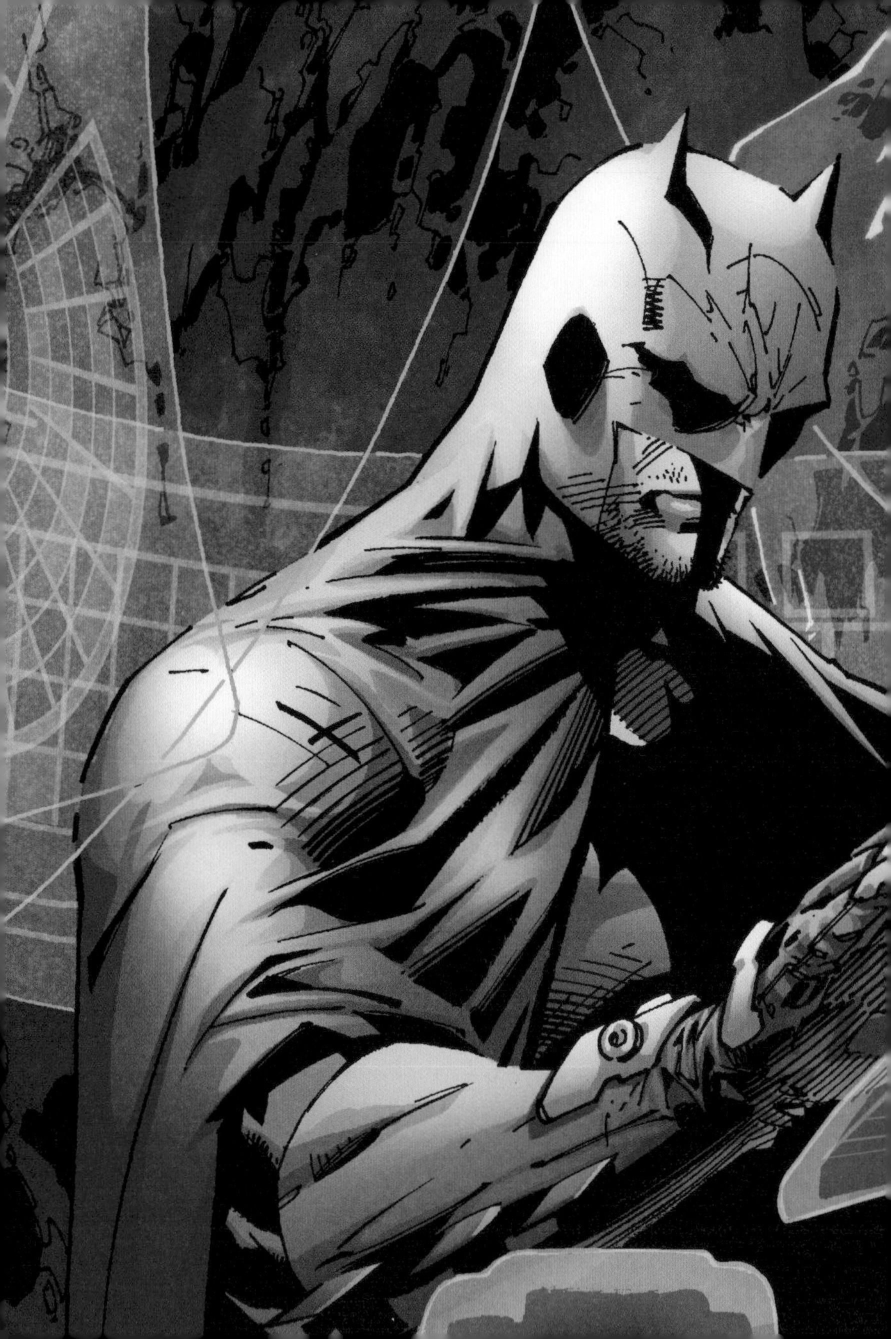

FIGHT SMART

Fighting evil isn't just about having the strength to land a knockout punch, it's about having the brains to win without breaking a sweat. Why patrol all over town looking for bad guys when you can hack into every CCTV camera in Gotham City and search the streets with your feet up? In your own daily life, a little thought will always give you the edge.

"It's like an Egyptian tomb now, testament to the greatness it represents."
Booster Gold

YOUR BASE IS YOUR BASIS FOR SUCCESS

They say "Home is where the heart is," but in Batman's case, home is where the Batcomputer is, and the helipad, and the Virtual Reality crime-scene simulator, and everything else he needs to succeed. For your own HQ, you don't need anything too fancy, just think practically. You'll need a space for your outfits, your secret files, your computer, and a hotline to your allies. And maybe a fridge.

"Sometimes, I admit, I think of Bruce as a man in a costume. Then, with some gadget from his Utility Belt, he reminds me... how lucky I am to be able to call on him."

Superman

HAVE THE BEST GADGETS

It's a fact: Batman's gadgets are better than anyone else's. More importantly, gadgets are cool. They impress the bad guys and make other heroes look cheap. They also save time and trouble. Why take the stairs when you can zoom up a Batrope? Why chase after a villain when you can hit them with a Batarang? Make sure you have the right gear to get you through any tricky situation.

"If detective work were easy...
everyone would be doing it."
Batman

ASK THE RIGHT QUESTIONS

If The Riddler is such a genius, why does he insist
on wearing that silly hat? If Robin didn't borrow the
Batmobile, where did those new dents come from?
The life of a crime fighter is full of mysteries. But so
is everyday life. Like where did your other sock go?
Who had the last chocolate cookie? Where did you
leave the remote? Like Batman, learn to ask the
really smart questions that get to the heart
of the matter.

"He does not provide solace from pain.
He cannot give you hope for the eternal…
Batman punches people in the face."
Bruce Wayne

KNOW YOUR STRENGTHS

Every hero has their strong points. Solving mysteries,
outwitting villains, driving an awesome car—that's
Batman stuff. Stopping aliens from invading Metropolis?
That's more Superman's style. Don't fight the wrong
battles. You'll just look silly. Grumpy squid? Leave it
to Aquaman. Something need lassoing? Try Wonder
Woman. Dangerous and alluring female cat-burglar
on the loose? Hey, that sounds like Batman again…
So, play to your strengths.

"Sometimes I think your *secrets* have secrets."
Robin

HAVE A SECRET SIDE

Being a legend means everyone wants a piece of you. But you'll go crazy if you don't get some privacy now and again. That's why Batman clings to his secret identity of billionaire Bruce Wayne. Now, *you* may not have another identity, but you can still keep some private space. Turn off your gadget. Sit on your own looking deep. Have a dark, secretive aspect, like never telling anyone your middle name.

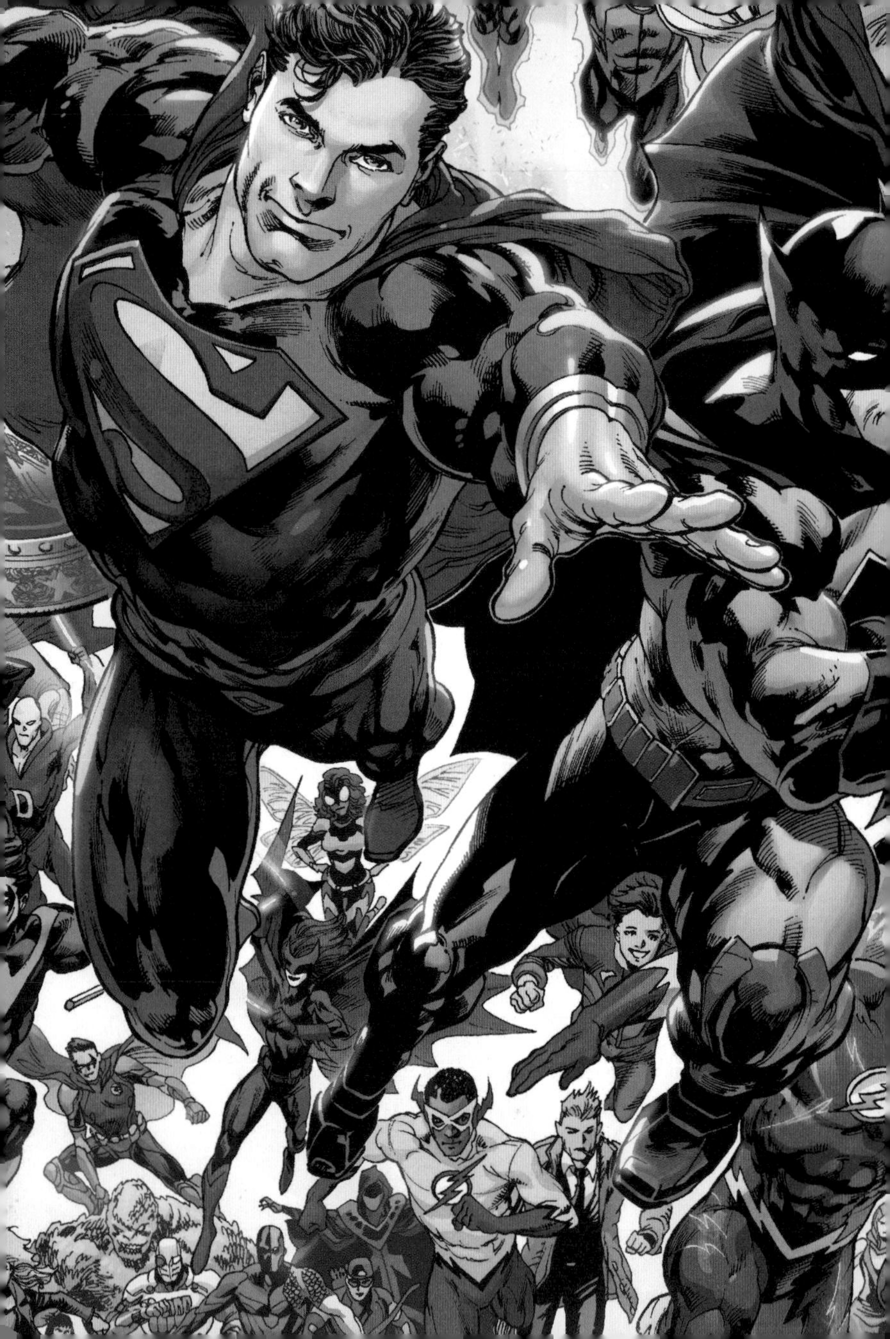

GET CONNECTED

Everyone has heard of Batman and his "one-man" war on crime. But for a loner, Batman sure has a lot of pals. What about Alfred Pennyworth, Robin, Nightwing, and Batgirl? Heroes need back-up, someone to help them if all their arch-enemies turn up at once. And so do you. As you go through life, put together your own Justice League of family, pals, and pets to see you through.

"I'm **not** whining! I live for adventure!
I revel in excitement!"
Robin

GET A SIDEKICK

Why does a hero as smart and tough as Batman
bother having a helper? Well, sidekicks like Robin are
vital—they can watch your back, distract enemies,
run errands, and best of all they make you look good
when you answer their questions. Just like Batman,
you can benefit from having a loyal ally. Saving the
world is more fun when you have someone to discuss
the best parts with after.

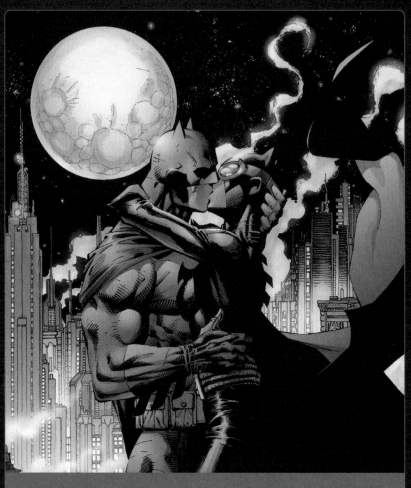

"I don't want to sound egotistical, Robin—but I've come to the conclusion that Catwoman is in love with me!"

Batman

KEEP FRIENDS CLOSE AND ENEMIES CLOSER

Batman benefits from having many Super Hero friends. But sometimes villains can come in useful too. The Penguin is a natural sneak and just loves to give away The Riddler's plans if he finds out about them. Catwoman started out as a villain but will always help Batman in a crisis (well, she has a crush on him). The lesson is, even if you see someone as an enemy, cut them a break sometimes, and see what they have to say—it may just surprise you.

"Deep down, Clark's a good person
… and deep down, I'm not."
Batman

BEFRIEND A SUPERHERO

Batman is used to being the star of the show, but
there is someone he is happy to share the headlines
with—Superman. He may not have a cool mask, but
the Man of Steel is bulletproof, can fly to the moon
and back if necessary, and can even turn back time—
which might come in useful if the Batmobile is parked
on a meter. You too can benefit from having pals like
this. Sometimes, even the toughest, smartest, or
coolest people around need a friend, so don't be
afraid to team up!

"I will say one thing for your nighttime activities—you do tend to **antagonize** the most interesting people."

Alfred Pennyworth

WORK WITH PEOPLE YOU CAN TRUST

Having high-flying heroes as pals is great. But when it comes to that person you depend on every day, make sure it is someone you can totally trust—someone who will give you an honest opinion. No one wants to be told they were a bit of a show-off, but that kind of remark keeps your feet on the ground. A true friend, like a good butler, will stand by you, even if you've spent a night in the sewers chasing after Killer Croc.

"Having friends, partners.
It all ends in betrayal and death."
Batman

DON'T GET DEPENDENT ON OTHERS

Despite all the advice in this chapter, sometimes you have to be able to handle stuff alone. Some things, like facing the dentist or taking an exam, have to be confronted solo. Even your best friend in the world might not be good to have around when you are on a romantic date. Robin can be brainwashed and Superman can be affected by Kryptonite. Train yourself to deal with some things on your own.

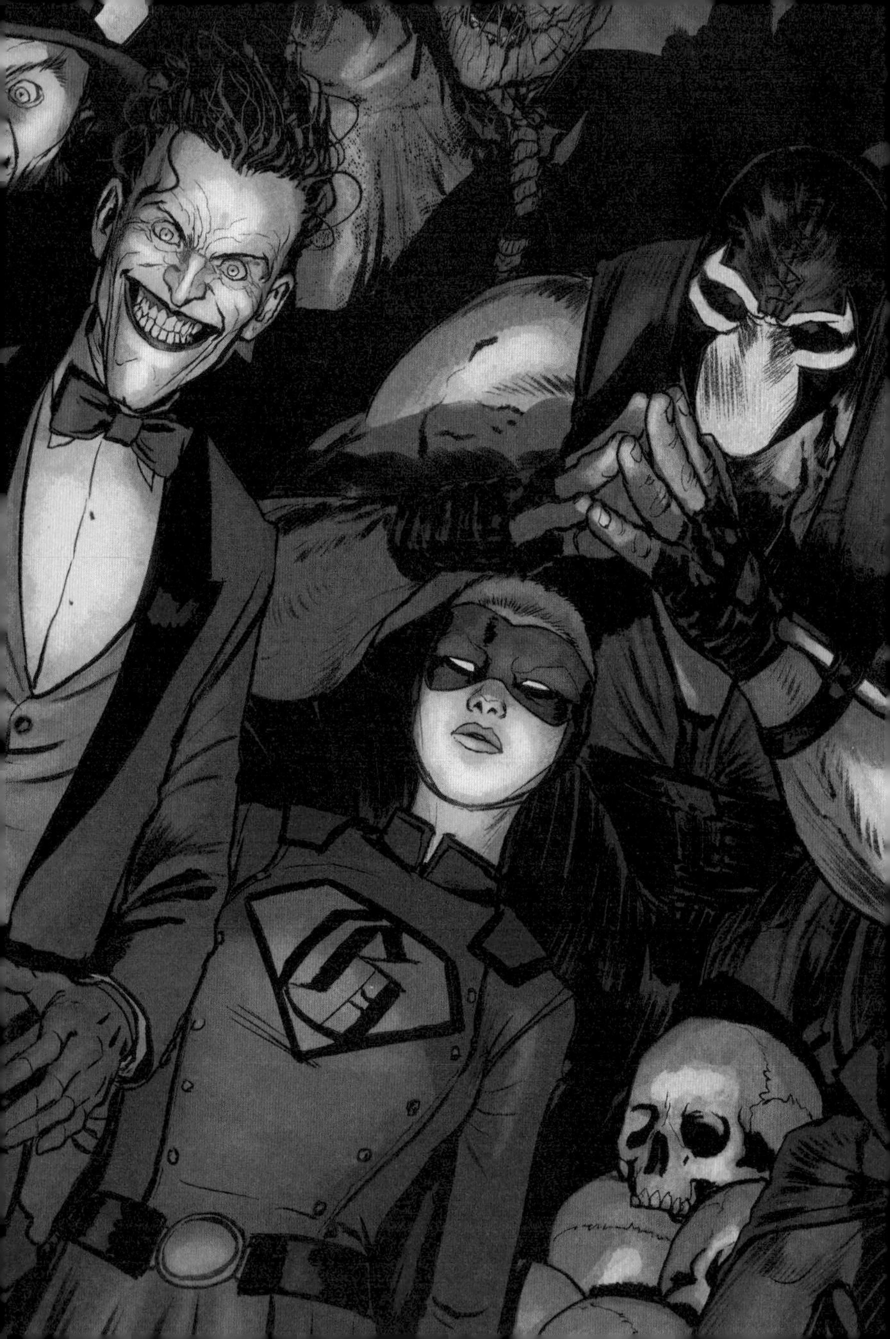

KNOW
YOUR ENEMIES

Batman realizes that to defeat his foes, he needs to know them inside out. Study them, and their weaknesses emerge. For example, Clayface slows down when he is cold, and appealing to The Joker's good side is a waste of time, because he doesn't have one. Similarly, you can learn about *your* enemies—the problems you face in life—to overcome them.

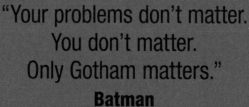

"Your problems don't matter.
You don't matter.
Only Gotham matters."

Batman

NEVER APPEAR WEAK TO YOUR FOES

How many times has Batman been caught in a deadly trap and left to perish? Countless. And how many times has he begged to be let out? Zero. Super-Villains do not respect weakness, and neither do life's many problems. Let on to your friends that you hate practical jokes and you'll be wearing a "kick me" sign in no time. So laugh at your troubles—it drives your enemies bonkers.

"It's over, Joker. Tell me where Pennyworth is and I'll only hurt you—a lot."

Batman

SPEAK YOUR ENEMIES' LANGUAGE

Try asking a Super-Villain nicely if they will stop being a menace to society, and they will laugh at you. No bad guy will ever burst into tears if you tell them you are disappointed in their actions. You will get better results with foul fiends if you sound as tough as them. Strong words can mask a decent personality, though—Batman may terrify his foes, but he would never stoop to their level.

"Action is what's called for.
Talking's for the birds."
Batman

ACTIONS SPEAK LOUDER THAN WORDS

Tell someone you are going to foil their plans and they won't believe you. Blow up their base by hacking into their orbiting death ray and they will be more impressed. Words can be hollow but a Batarang sure isn't. If you plan to do something cool, don't message all your friends to boast about it in advance. Just go ahead and do it. They'll be a lot more impressed by hearing that you've climbed Everest, than by you telling them you've bought climbing gear.

"'Criminal mastermind' and *you*
don't come together immediately."
Batman

KEEP YOUR ENEMIES IN THEIR PLACE

If you call some persistent villain your "greatest foe" they are sure to keep coming up with evil plans, just to keep top position. But tell them you scarcely give them a second thought and you will make them feel small. Batman keeps criminals in place by defeating them and embarrassing them in the process. Like the Dark Knight, you can keep your enemies in their place with just a witty word here and there.

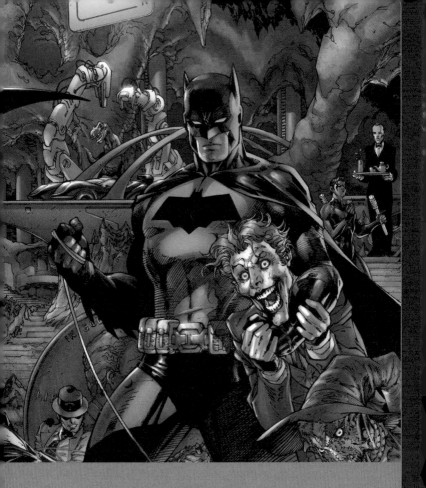

"Leave them alone, Joker.
This is between you and me."
Batman

MAKE IT PERSONAL

Batman knows that while villains are targeting him they are not tormenting innocent bystanders. That's why he makes it personal. Sometimes bad guys get so preoccupied with hating Batman they forget to follow their plans properly. You can create an impact by making things personal too. Your opponent may get so riled up that they make a critical mistake.

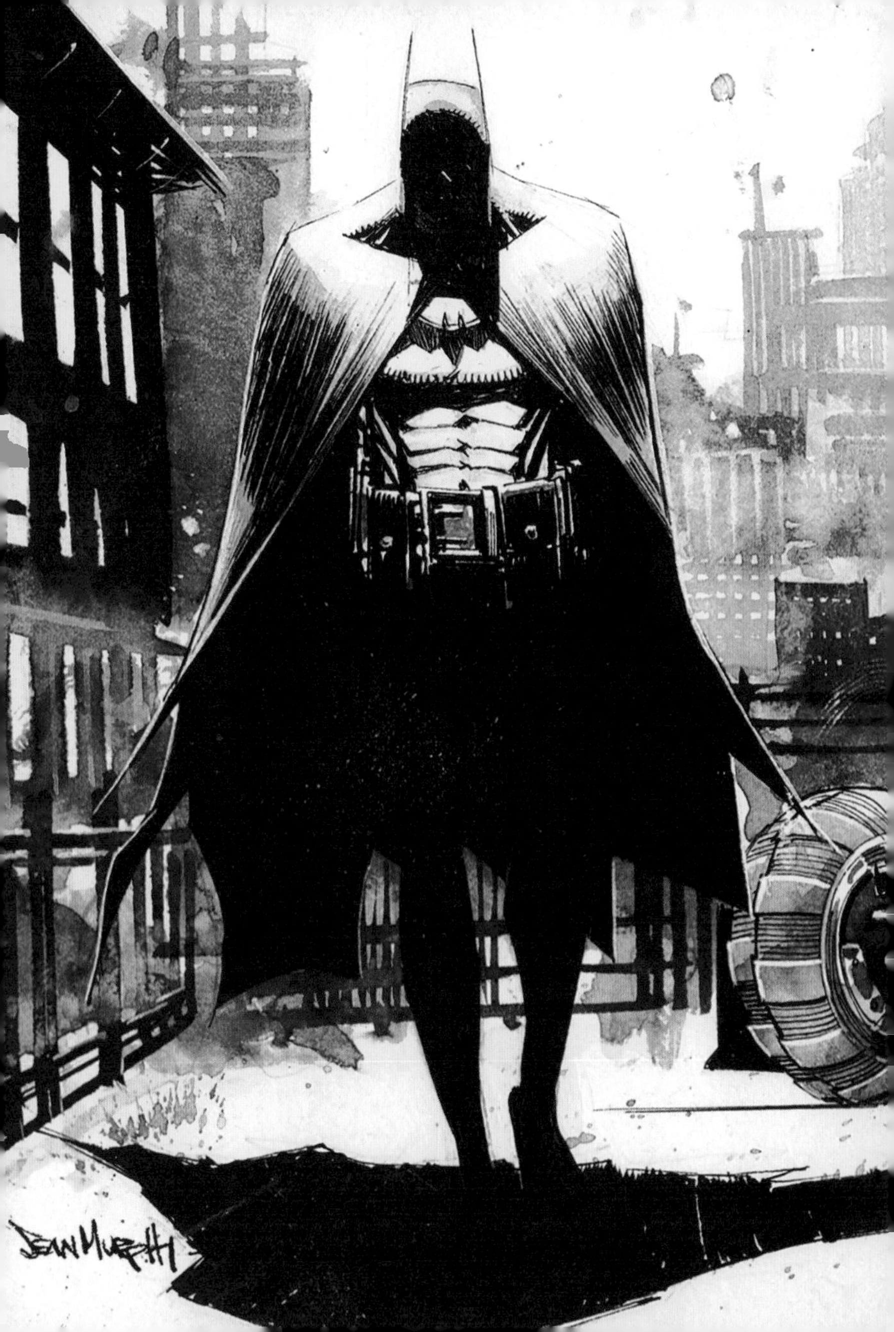

BECOME A LEGEND

One simple thing helps Batman to keep crime down in Gotham City—the fact that he is a legend. It makes foes think twice about tackling him. It scares punks and hired henchmen. No one knows where the truth ends and the legend begins. You can become a legend too, by pushing yourself to achieve things that no one thinks you can do.

"I wear a mask. And that mask, it's not to hide **who** I am, but to create **what** I am."

Batman

YOU *ARE* THE MISSION

To get where you want, don't just have a mission, become the mission. Your goal in life is not just something you do on Wednesday afternoons if it isn't raining—it's what you live and breathe 24/7. If Batman only fought crime on the nights when there was nothing good on TV, then the underworld would soon learn to work around him. Don't just have a dream—become that dream.

"All men have limits. They learn what they are and learn not to exceed them. I ignore mine."
Batman

MIND OVER MATTER

The Dark Knight is often driven to his limits but has learned to go beyond. You can't tell Bane you won't fight him because you have a bad back. You have to learn to keep going. Batman isn't superhuman, but he expands the idea of what a human can achieve. Maybe expand your idea of yourself. Next time you face an impossible challenge, just put on your Batman voice and say, "I'm on it!"

"Maybe that's what Batman is about. Not winning. But failing, and getting back up."

Bruce Wayne

GET BACK UP

Anyone can fail at something. The heroic part is getting back up again. Sometimes it's hard to get back up—you feel a failure and you lack confidence. But when you're on your feet again, you're stronger. You're stronger because you learn from your mistakes. Every defeat is a chance to amaze the world at your resilience. Bounce back, pull your cowl on again, and say: "I'm Batman!"

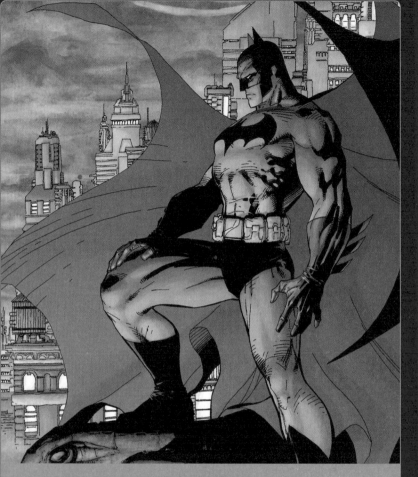

"It won't do any good for me to
allow my emotions to gain control…
not while there's a job ahead!"

Batman

STAY CALM

True legends have quiet confidence. They stay
cool in a crisis. Learn to control your feelings and
calmly get on with the job: Batman doesn't anxiously
bite his fingernails before a battle, and he doesn't
punch the air after beating The Joker. He takes it all
in stride. It's the coolest way to be, and it's much
better for your nerves.

"I'm not done yet. Not while Gotham City needs Batman. Not until the night's over."

Bruce Wayne

BE SURE OF
YOUR DESTINY

By now you should be ready for your mission.
You don't have to be the World's Greatest Detective to
follow the clues we've given you. You'll be the hero
you want to be if you follow your destiny. Pull your
cape on and don't look back. Remember, the world
needs heroes, and you have all you need to become
one. Like Bruce Wayne, you may have no amazing
superpowers, but you have the desire to
Be More Batman, and that is enough.

Senior Editor David Fentiman
Project Art Editor Jon Hall
Production Editor Siu Yin Chan
Senior Production Controller Louise Minihane
Managing Editor Sarah Harland
Managing Art Editor Vicky Short
Publishing Director Mark Searle

DK would like to thank: Benjamin Harper and Josh Anderson at Warner Bros.
Consumer Products; Mike Pallotta, Doug Prinzivalli, Leah Tuttle,
and Joseph Daley at DC Comics.

First American Edition, 2021
Published in the United States by DK Publishing
1450 Broadway, Suite 801, New York, NY 10018

Page design copyright © 2021
Dorling Kindersley Limited
DK, a Division of Penguin Random House LLC
21 22 23 24 25 10 9 8 7 6 5 4 3 2 1
001–321226–May/2021

A catalog record for this book is available
from the Library of Congress.
ISBN 978-0-7440-2852-2

DK books are available at special discounts when
purchased in bulk for sales promotions, premiums,
fund-raising, or educational use.
For details, contact:
DK Publishing Special Markets,
1450 Broadway, Suite 801, New York, NY 10018
SpecialSales@dk.com

Printed and bound in China

For the curious
www.dk.com

ARTIST ACKNOWLEDGMENTS
Brian Bolland, Norm Breyfogle, Greg Capullo,
Andy Clarke, Tony S. Daniel, Jason Fabok,
David Finch, Sandu Florea, Jorge Fornés,
Richard Friend, Lee Garbet, Tomás Giorello,
Patrick Gleason, Mick Gray, Scott Hanna, Mikel Janín,
Jim Lee, Clay Mann, Dave Mazzucchelli, Tomeu
Morey, Win Mortimer, Sean Murphy, Yasmine Putri,
Tim Sale, Ira Schnapp, Anthony Tollin, Scott Williams

The publishers have made every effort to identify
and acknowledge the artists whose work appears
in this book.

MIX
Paper from
responsible sources
FSC™ C018179

This book is made from
Forest Stewardship Council™
certified paper—one small
step in DK's commitment
to a sustainable future.

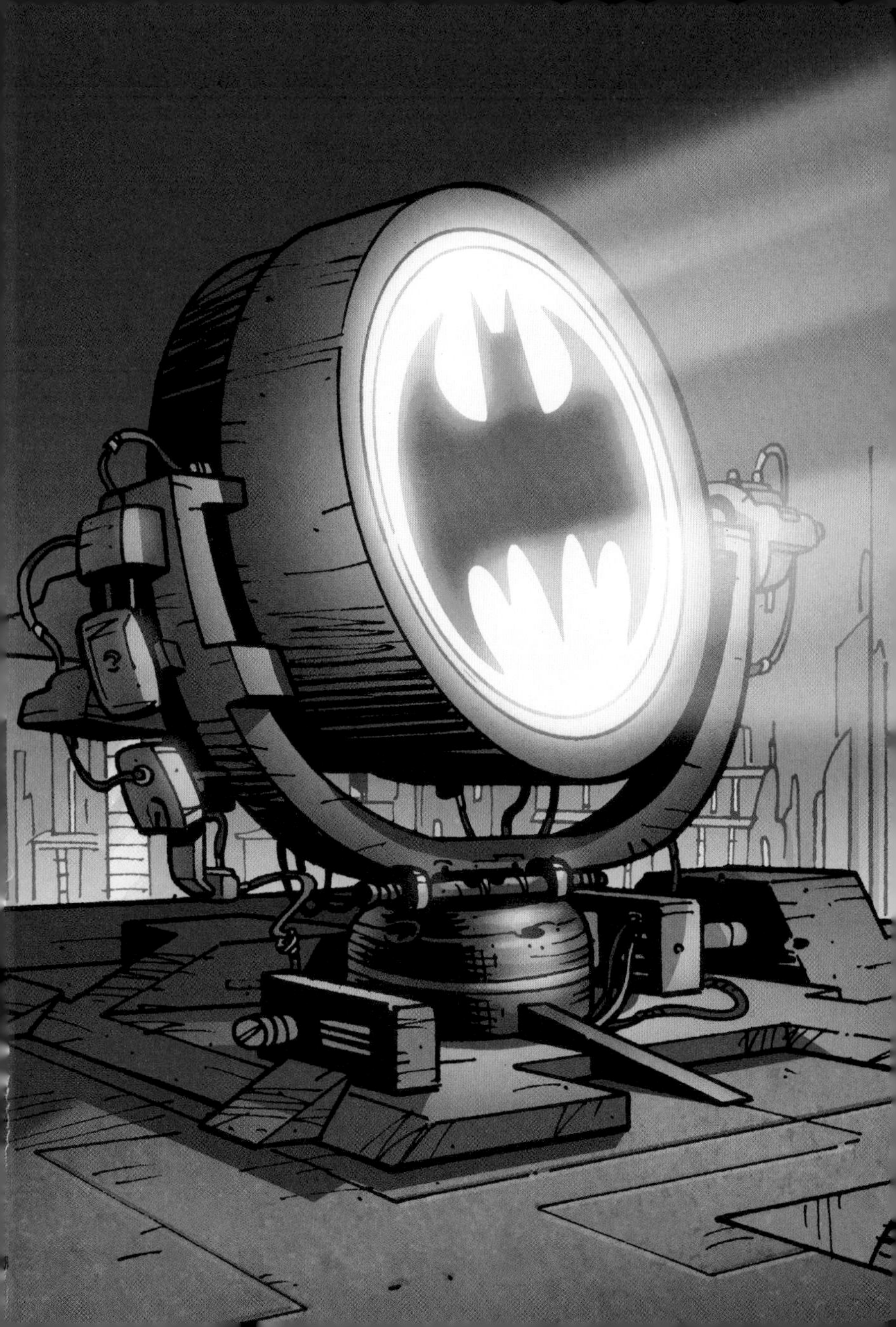